Sportsviewers Guide
TENNIS

Reginald Brace

DAVID & CHARLES
Newton Abbot   London

Contents

History and development   4–7
How the real tennis played by Henry VIII was simplified and revised by two Victorian army majors. Why the Marylebone Cricket Club was called in to write the rules and why the first Wimbledon champion thought little of the event.

Rules and terminology   8–17
The fundamental rules of the game including a glossary of terms.

The stars   18–41
An A–Z of the game's current leading players from Jimmy Arias to Mats Wilander, among the men, and from Tracy Austin to Virginia Wade, among the women.

Road to the top   42–43
How the top players reach the highest peaks from local junior tournaments to international world stars.

Equipment   44–45
A guide to some of the top players' rackets and what they earn from wearing other kit.

Technique   46–47
The key shots in the game are described and illustrations show how these shots are executed by the top players.

Events and competitions   48–51
This includes a tour of the top circuits — WCT and Grand Prix — with a look at the four majors (the championships of Wimbledon, Australia, France and the United States).

Venues   52–57
The world's main theatres of tennis are described, with a special look at the history and development of Wimbledon.

People in the media   58–59
The men behind the familiar voices of Dan Maskell, John Barrett and Mark Cox are brought to life.

Statistics   60–64

British Library Cataloguing in Publication Data
Brace, Reginald
  Tennis. — (Sportsviewers guides)
  1. Tennis
  I. Title   II. Series
  796.342   GV995

ISBN 0-7153-8537-2

The Sportsviewers' Guide to Tennis was produced and designed by
Siron Publishing Limited of
20 Queen Anne Street, London W1
Series editor: Nicholas Keith
Photographs by Tommy Hindley and Tony Henshaw of Professional Sport
Designed by Ann Doolan
Cartoons by Des Marwood

© David & Charles (Publishers) Ltd 1984. All rights reserved. No part of this publication may be reproduced, stored in a retrieval system or transmitted in any form or by any means, electronic, mechanical, photocopying, recording or otherwise, without prior permission of David & Charles (Publishers) Limited.

Typeset by ABM Typographics Ltd, Hull and printed by
Printer Industria Gráfica SA
Cuatro Caminos, Apartado 8,
Sant Vincenç dels Horts,
Barcelona, Spain   DLB 36115-1983
for David & Charles (Publishers) Limited
Brunel House   Newton Abbot   Devon

Foreword

Sports develop a language of their own. Tennis is no exception. What is a point penalty, a chop, the ATP, a seed, Roland Garros? Words full of significance to the tennis world but unfamiliar often to the most avid viewer or spectator.

With this book 'Sportsviewers Guide to Tennis' Reg Brace has provided the answer. He has produced an excellent reference work. A balanced mixture of fundamental information about the history of the game, the rules, advice on equipment and insights into techniques and styles of play. This is supported with a wealth of intriguing material, both biographical and topical, about the stars participating in the modern game and the tournaments in which they compete.

His concise constructive comments ensure that the reader can gain the maximum amount of information in the shortest possible time. It is hardly surprising that Reg Brace has such a feel for the game as his international journalistic career has made him a familiar figure on the tennis scene for over a quarter of a century.

This comprehensive guide will not only instruct the uninitiated but will also make a valuable contribution to the enthusiast. It will certainly be a mandatory companion for the commentator!

Mark Cox

History and development

The ancient Romans and Greeks played a form of tennis, if we are placing the correct interpretation on their mosaics, statues and learned writings. The medieval French slapped a ball back and forth with their hands and called the pastime *jeu de paume*.

King Henry VIII, it is said, rose at five in the morning to play tennis in an enclosed court at Hampton Court Palace which is used today. He had his own professional, Anthony Ansley, who supplied balls and rackets and apparently kept score. The game which King Hal played with the gusto he brought to his other favourite sport is now known as real tennis. It is still played by a small but loyal following using the same curiously shaped indoor court, lopsided rackets and balls made of compressed cloth with a hand-stitched felt cover.

Real tennis took shape as a popular game for clerics in the cloisters of French monasteries. It was described by twelfth century writers and, along with its strange trappings, the game retains its original French names ('dedans', 'grille', 'tambour') to this day. Lawn tennis, the outdoor version of this esoteric pursuit, came into prominence in the 19th century. The man who is often described as its inventor was Major Walter Clopton Wingfield although he cannot be given the entire credit because there were other pioneer innovators whom history cannot ignore.

Major Wingfield was a retired Army officer, a magistrate for the county of Montgomeryshire and a member of the corps of Gentlemen-at-Arms at the court of Queen Victoria. He published a book of rules in December 1873 and two months later applied for a patent for 'A New and Portable Court for Playing the Ancient Game of Tennis' which was granted in July 1874.

The sporting Major called his game *Sphairistike,* which could have been his biggest mistake in selling it to the general public. This Greek word for ball game was soon abbreviated to

Tea on the lawns at Wimbledon in 1905 (BBC Hulton Picture Library).

'Sticky' and eventually abandoned in favour of lawn tennis which was easier to pronounce and remember.

The game came in a painted box containing poles, pegs and netting for creating a court, four tennis bats, a supply of hollow India rubber balls, a mallet and brush and a book of rules. It cost five guineas and was designed to be played on grass — ideally, advised the Major, on frosty days when the best of the shooting was over and the ground was too hard for hunting.

The story goes that the game was first played at a house party in Nantclwyd in December 1873. It would be easy to describe this as the birth of lawn tennis but it is not as simple as that. There is firm evidence that lawn tennis was played at Edgbaston in 1858 and subsequently at the Manor House Hotel, Leamington, where a plaque states: 'On this lawn in 1872 the first lawn tennis club in the world was founded'.

Major Harry Gem and Mr J. B. Perera were the initiators here and in a technical sense their case is strengthened by the fact that their court was rectangular, unlike that of Major Wingfield's which was in the shape of an hour-glass. The rules of their game were compiled by Gem and it is fairer to link the two Majors — Gem and Wingfield — when it comes to awarding the credit for launching lawn tennis.

Croquet, a deeply entrenched English summer pastime, was quickly rivalled in popularity by the new game. Other manufacturers moved in with different sets of rules and it was obvious that some standardisation was necessary if lawn tennis was not to bewilder its exponents.

This was where the Marylebone Cricket Club intervened. The MCC's tennis and rackets sub-committee had made a brave job of revising the rules

William and Ernest Renshaw (BBC Hulton Picture Library).

Lottie Dod: champion at 15 (BBC Hulton Picture Library).

5

History and development/2

of real tennis so it seemed logical that the same body should try to introduce a common code of play for the brash interloper called lawn tennis.

A meeting was held at Lord's on 3 March 1875 and as a result new and agreed rules were published on 29 May. A significant innovation was that the service should be delivered with one foot behind the baseline and alternatively into the two sides of the court between the net and the service line. Scoring was up to 15 with deuce-advantage at 14-14.

It was an important step towards uniformity but a far more momentous development occurred in 1877. The All-England Croquet Club, which had embraced lawn tennis, decided to stage a tournament at its ground at Worple Road, Wimbledon — principally to raise money for the repair of a pony-roller.

The MCC's rules were a diplomatic compromise which left room for numerous variations. In a tournament with a cup worth twenty-five guineas at stake and competitors paying one guinea for the privilege of playing, there had to be tighter control.

A committee made up of Henry Jones, Julian Marshall and C. H. Heathcote were entrusted with the job and they came up with rules which have held — give or take a few minor changes — to the present day. They decreed that the court should be rectangular, 78 feet long and 27 feet wide, and that tennis scoring should be used. The foundations of lawn tennis as we know it now were laid.

This was the world's first lawn tennis tournament and the birth of Wimbledon, which remains the centrepiece of the game. There was only

Suzanne Lenglen: six titles (BBC Hulton Picture Library).

Reggie and Laurie Doherty (BBC Hulton Picture Library).

one event, the men's singles, and it was won from an entry of 22 by Spencer W. Gore when he beat William Marshall 6–1 6–2 6–4. A profit of £10 ensured the future of the pony-roller but the first Wimbledon champion was hardly enthusiastic about the future of lawn tennis.

'It is its want of variety that will prevent lawn tennis in its present form from taking rank among our great games,' wrote Gore in 1890. 'That anyone who has played really well at cricket, tennis or even rackets will ever seriously give his attention to lawn tennis beyond showing himself to be a promising player is extremely doubtful, for in all probability the monotony of the game as compared with the others would choke him off before he had time to excel in it.'

Frank Hadow, who used his leave from the coffee plantations of Ceylon to beat Gore and win the second Wimbledon championships the following year, was hardly an encouraging advertisement for the new game either. After defeating Gore's net-rushing by cunning use of the lob he returned to Ceylon and never played lawn tennis again.

But if the first two Wimbledon champions were less than enthused by the game, the seeds of lawn tennis as an international addiction had taken root. An American, Mary Outerbridge, succumbed to the game in Bermuda where it was played by the British garrison and constructed a court on Staten Island, New York, in 1874. Two years later a Bostonian, Dr James Dwight, won a tournament at Nahany, Massachusetts.

Lawn tennis had crossed the Atlantic. Despite the dismissive attitude of its first two titleholders, Wimbledon was on its way to becoming one of the world's great sporting occasions.

Rules and terminology

The basic rules of tennis are clear and easy to understand. This is one of the attractions of the game. Here it is necessary to record only the more important points from the rule book, as administered by the International Tennis Federation. Some of them are obvious, but it does no harm to set them out.

The court
The bounds of the court are shown in the accompanying diagram. It must be remembered that under Rule 22 a 'ball falling on a line is regarded as falling in the court bounded by that line.'

Tennis involves games and sets. To win a game a player must win five points and be two points ahead. A set is won by the player who first reaches six games and is two games ahead. In the past if the players reached five games all they continued the set until one was two games ahead. This led to some extremely long sets — the record number of games in a set is

The ball
The ball must have a uniform outer surface and must be white or yellow in colour. If there are any seams they have to be stitchless (Rule 3). The ball must be more than 2½in (6.35cm) and less than 2⅝in (6.67cm) in diameter, and more than 2oz (56.7 grams) and less than 2¹/₁₆oz (58.5 grams) in weight. The ball must have a bound of more than 53in (135cm) and less than 58in (147cm) when dropped 100in (254cm) upon a concrete base.

There are also precise specifications about the ball's 'deformation', i.e. the effects of impact. Balls are changed after every nine games — seven games in the first instance because new balls are used in the knock-up before a match begins.

The racket
Rackets failing to comply with the following specifications are not approved (Rule 4):

(a) The hitting surface of the racket must be flat and consist of a pattern of crossed strings connected to a frame and alternately interlaced or bonded where they cross; and the stringing pattern must be generally uniform.

(b) The frame of the racket cannot exceed 32in (81.28cm) in overall length, including the handle and 12½in (31.75cm) in overall width. The strung surface must not exceed 15½in (39.37cm) in overall length, and 11½in (29.21cm) in overall width.

(c) The frame, including the handle and the strings:
'(i) shall be free of attached objects and protrusions, other than those utilised solely and specifically to limit or prevent wear and tear or vibration, or to distribute weight, and which are reasonable in size and placement for such purposes;

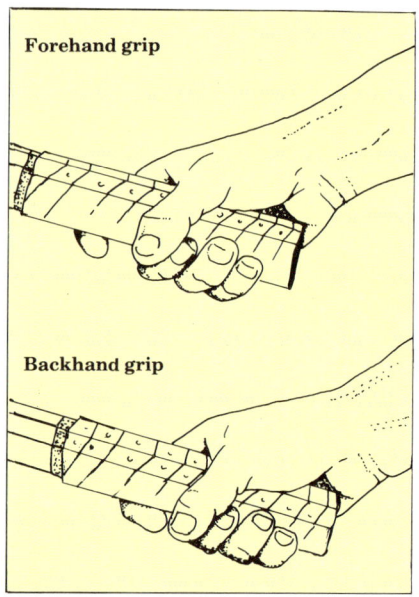

Forehand grip

Backhand grip

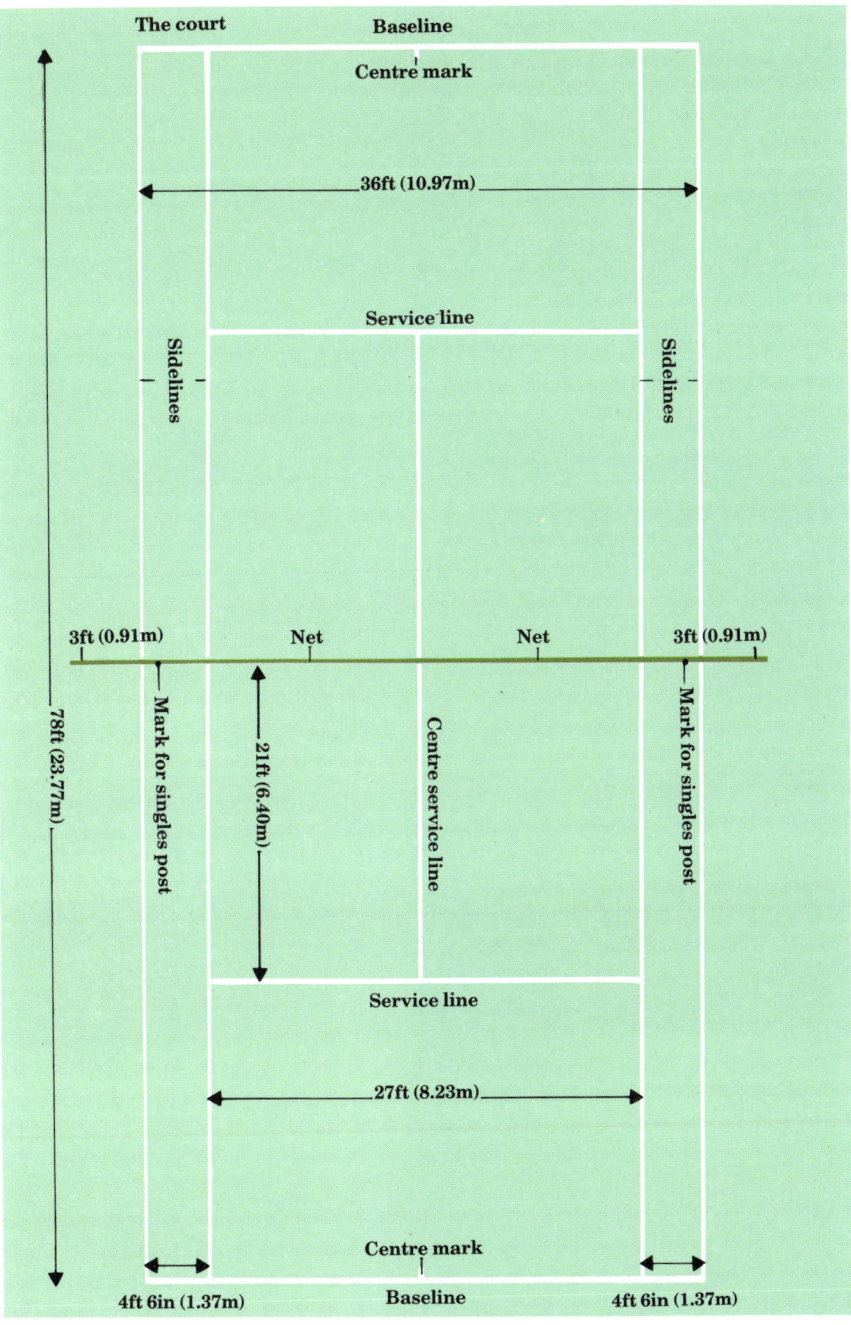

Rules and terminology/2

(ii) shall be free of any device which makes it possible for a player to change materially the shape of the racket.'

Serving
Rule 5 is quite straightforward and deals with server and receiver. The players stand on opposite sides of the net — as you will have noticed on TV! — and the player who first delivers the ball is called the server and the other the receiver.

The choice of ends and the right to be server or receiver in the first game is decided by toss (Rule 6).

(a) The right to be server or receiver in which case the other player chooses the end, or

(b) The end, in which case the other player chooses the right to be server or receiver.

Before serving, the server must stand with both feet at rest behind (i.e. further from the net than) the baseline and within the imaginary continuations of the centre mark and the sideline (Rule 7). 'The server shall then project the ball by hand into the air in any direction and before it hits the ground strike it with his racket and the delivery shall be deemed to have been completed at the moment of the impact of the racket and the ball. A player with the use of only one arm may utilise his racket for the projection.'

Foot faults (Rule 8): 'The server shall throughout the delivery of the service:

(a) Not change his position by walking or running.

(b) Not touch, with either foot, any area other than that behind the baseline within the imaginary extension of the centre mark and side line.'

The server must stand alternately behind the right and left courts, beginning from the right in every game (Rule 9). If a serve is made from a

A selection of rackets.

wrong half of the court and is undetected, subsequent play stands, but the inaccuracy must be corrected immediately it is discovered. The service ball has to pass over the net and hit the ground within the service court which is diagonally opposite or upon any line bounding such court before the receiver returns it.

Faults (Rule 10): The service is a fault if the server commits any breach of rules 7, 8 or 9; if he misses the ball in attempting to strike it; if the ball served touches a permanent fixture (other than the net, strap or band) before it hits the ground.

Sometimes a let is called (Rule 13) because of an interruption in play or a dispute over a decision by a linesman. In that case the point is replayed.

However, a serve is a let: '(a) If the ball served touches the net, strap or band and is otherwise good, or, after touching the net, strap or band touches the receiver or anything which he wears or carries before hitting the ground; (b) If service or a fault happens when the receiver is not ready.'

The tie-break

The tie-break was introduced to streamline the game and bring it into line with modern tastes. It meant the end of inordinately long matches like the 112 game contest at Wimbledon in 1969 between Pancho Gonzales and Charlie Pasarell, which Gonzales won 22–24 1–6 16–14 6–3 11–9. A nine-point method was used at the US Open in 1970. This was introduced at six games all in games and could be settled by a 'sudden death' point if the score went to four points all.

Wimbledon adopted the less dramatic twelve-point system in 1971. Here the tie-break is won by the first player to reach seven points providing he is at least two points ahead. A lead of two points must be established if the score reaches six points all. The twelve-point tie-break subsequently became part of the rules in tennis as an optional scoring method, usually brought into operation at six games all.

The player whose turn it is to serve serves the first point. His opponent serves the next two points and thereafter each player serves alternately for two consecutive points. From the first point, each service is delivered alternately from the right and left courts beginning from the right court.

Players change ends after every six points and at the conclusion of the tie-break game. (The tie-break counts as one game for the ball change except that if the balls are due to be changed at the beginning of the tie-break the change is delayed until the second game of the following set.)

In doubles the same tie-break rules apply. The player whose turn it is to serve serves the first point. Thereafter each player serves in rotation for two points, in the same order as previously in that set. The player (or pair in the case of doubles) who served first in the tie-break game receives service in the first game of the following set.

Time allowed

A maximum of thirty seconds is allowed from the moment the ball goes out of play at the end of one point to the time the ball is struck for the next point. When changing ends a maximum of one minute thirty seconds is permitted. The umpire can use his discretion when there is interference which makes it impossible for the server to serve within that time.

Rules and terminology/3

Penalties

The point penalty procedure under the code of conduct drawn up by the Men's International Professional Tennis Council (MIPTC) is:

First offence	Warning
Second offence	Point
Third offence	Game
Fourth offence	Default

In MIPTC-sanctioned tournaments, and Davis Cup or King's Cup matches when a neutral umpire has been appointed, point penalties are levied by the umpire. In the event of an umpire failing to levy a point penalty for a code violation, the referee or the MIPTC supervisor may order him to do so. In Davis Cup and King's Cup matches when a neutral umpire has not been appointed, the referee of MIPTC supervisor determines code violations and instructs the chair umpire to impose any point penalties.

Ilie Nastase: often clashed with tournament officials.

Glossary of terms

Ace A winning serve which the receiver fails to touch.
Advantage The point which follows deuce. In tournament play umpires usually call the name of the player holding advantage, e.g. 'Advantage Smith'; in doubles the server or receiver. At a more informal level the advantage is often shortened to 'van'.
All In tennis this word means an even score. Within a game 15–15 is 15–all and 30–30 is 30–all. In a set a level game score is called one–all, two–all, three–all.
All England Club The venue for Wimbledon.
Approach shot The drive hit by a player which precedes his advance to the net.
ATP Association of Tennis Professionals: the male touring professionals' union.
ATP computer rankings A ranking system based on the results of every male touring player.

Backhand The shot hit from the opposite side to the hand holding the racket.
Baseline The back line of a tennis court.
Baseliner A player who operates from the back of the court.
Break The loss of a service game by the server.
Break point The receiver's chance to break service. Break points are love–40, 15–40, 30–40 and advantage receiver.
Centre Court The main court in any tennis arena, although Wimbledon's Centre Court is the most celebrated in the game.
Chip A short, sliced shot, also called a dink, designed to outwit the incoming volleyer.

Rules and terminology/4

Chop A stroke which imparts underspin to the ball.

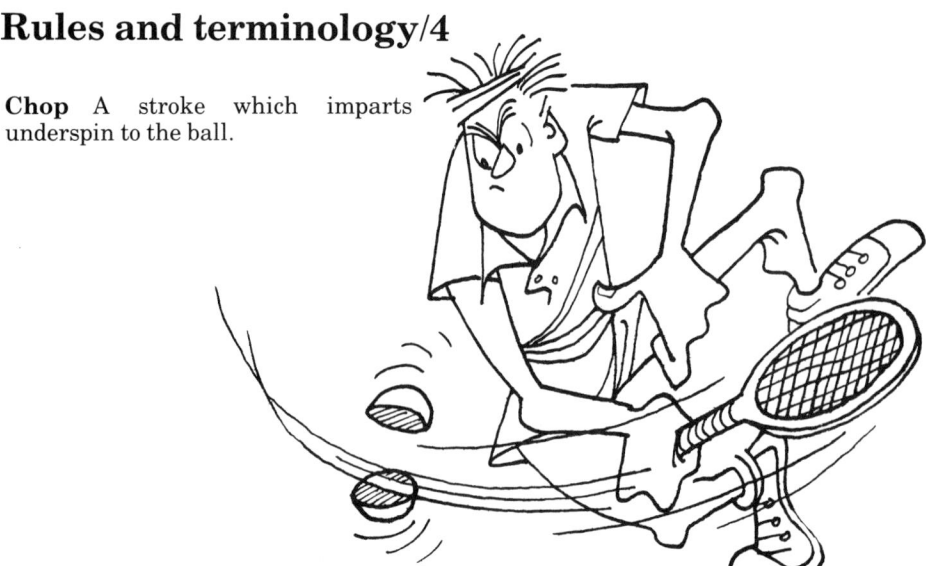

Court Where tennis is played. Surfaces vary in composition and speed but the dimensions are always the same: 78 feet long and 27 feet wide for singles; 36 feet wide for doubles.
Cross-court A shot hit diagonally across the court.
Davis Cup The premier men's team competition in international tennis, first held in 1900.
Deuce The term used when the game score is 40–all.
Double fault Two consecutive service errors to lose the point.
Drop shot A soft, short shot designed to catch an opponent off guard.

Elbow 'Getting the elbow' means tightening up under pressure. Tennis elbow is a painful physical condition.
Federation Cup The women's equivalent of the Davis Cup.
Flushing Meadow New York home of the US Open.
Foot fault An infringement by the server when he steps on the baseline or serves from the wrong side of the centre line.
Forecourt The court between the net and the service line.
Forehand The shot hit from the same side as the hand holding the racket.
Foro Italico The site of the Italian championships in Rome.
Game A game comprises four points: 15, 30, 40 and game unless it is tied at deuce, or 40–all, when a player must win two clear points to win the game. The next scoring unit after a game is a set.
Grand Prix A linked series of men's tournaments held between January and December and embracing all the major championships.

Grand Slam Winning the four leading championships (Wimbledon, US, French and Australian) in a year. Only four players have done this: Don Budge (1938), Maureen Connolly (1953), Rod Laver (1962 and 1969) and Margaret Court (1970).

Grip Usually one-handed with variations (Eastern, Western, Continental) although a number of players (notably Borg, Connors and Chris Lloyd) have excelled using two hands.

Ground-stroke A shot from the back of the court after the ball has bounced.

Half-volley Returning the ball immediately after it strikes the ground.

ITF The International Tennis Federation, the game's governing body.

King's Cup The international men's indoor team championship of Europe.

Rules and terminology/5

LTA Lawn Tennis Association the governing body of British tennis.
Let The term used for a replayed point.
Lob A stroke that goes above the opponent's head.
Love Means nought.
Masters The play-off climax to the Grand Prix.
Match A tennis contest. Duration may be best of three sets or best of five sets.
Rally The exchange of shots which decides a point.
Referee The official in charge of a tournament.
Roland Garros The stadium in Paris where the French Open is held.
Rubber A singles or doubles match in a team competition.
Seeding Separating the leading players in a tournament so that they do not clash in early rounds. If the seedings follow form the top two seeds should meet in the final.

MIPTC Men's International Professional Tennis Council. The ruling body of the men's professional game, comprising representatives of the ITF, ATP and tournaments.
Mixed doubles A doubles with a man and a woman on each side.
Net cord A shot which strikes the top of the net before dropping into court. Also the cord or cable which supports the net.
Not up A familiar umpiring call when the ball is judged to have been struck after the second bounce.
Overhead Another word for the smash, a stroke executed with a service action.
Passing shot A shot which avoids the reach of the volleyer.
Service The shot which begins every tennis rally. The server has two chances to hit the ball diagonally into his rival's service court.
Service line The line between the net and the baseline.
Service winner A service which might be touched by the receiver but is not returned over the net.
Set The first to reach six games wins a set unless the score is 5–5. Then a two game margin is required except when the tie-break is employed, usually at 6–6. The tie-break ends the set, with the score reading 7–6.
Set point The point which can decide a set.

Sideline The lines at each side of the court marking the boundary for singles and doubles.
Slice A stroke which imparts underspin to the ball.
Smash The stroke which answers the lob executed with a service action.

United States begun in 1923 and held annually with each country taking it in turn to stage the tie.
Wimbledon The game's premier tournament first held in 1877. To be a Wimbledon champion is to carry the most coveted accolade in tennis.

Throat The part of a tennis racket between the head and the handle.
Tie-break A device for ending a tied set, usually introduced at 6–6. Also known as the tie-breaker. The first player to win seven points wins the game and the set provided he leads by a margin of two points. If the score reaches 6–6 the tie-break continues until the two point margin has been achieved.
Topspin The opposite to underspin achieved by striking over the top of the ball from low to high.
Tramline The area between the singles and doubles sidelines.
Umpire The official in charge of a match.
Volley Striking the ball before it bounces.
WCT World Championship Tennis: promoters of professional tennis.
Wightman Cup A women's team competition between Britain and the

WTA Women's Tennis Association, the union of professional women tennis players.

The Stars

Men

Jimmy Arias (US)

Jimmy Arias became the second youngest player to win the Italian Open in May 1983 with a victory over the Spaniard José Higueras which did a world of good for his confidence and his computer ranking. He was 18 — a year older than Bjorn Borg when the Swede captured the title in 1974.

Born on 16 August 1964 at Grand Island, New York, Arias shares an unusual record with a fellow American, Andrea Jaeger, in that they are the youngest winners of a major open championship. Jimmy was 16 years 296 days and Andrea was 15 years 339 days when they captured the mixed doubles title at the French Open in June 1981. Arias is a tenacious and intelligent player whose strongest shot is a penetrating forehand struck with a Western grip. Further evidence of his rapidly developing talent came in the 1983 US Open when he defeated Yannick Noah to reach the semi-finals, where he was overpowered by Ivan Lendl in straight sets.

Bjorn Borg (Sweden)

Although there are periodic rumours of a comeback, Bjorn Borg officially retired from circuit competition at the Monte Carlo Open in March 1983. Borg beat José-Luis Clerc in the first round but was then ushered into retirement by Henri Leconte who defeated him 4–6 7–5 7–6.

Although he was aged only 26 at the time, Bjorn had done enough to rank among the greatest players in the history of the game. His record of five consecutive Wimbledon titles (1976–80) and six French (1974–75 and 1978–81) was an incredible achievement, unlikely to be equalled. Born in Sodertalje, Sweden, on 6 June 1956, he started playing tennis at the age of 9 and made his Davis Cup debut when he was 15. Four years later he led Sweden to victory in the competition.

In a marvellous career, characterised by stirring matches and glittering triumphs, the only major title to escape him was the US Open in which he was runner-up in 1976, 1978, 1980 and 1981. The first hints of disenchantment with tennis came in 1982 when he took a break and was told he would have to qualify for Grand Prix tournaments after declining to compete in the required number of events.

Borg understandably thought he was a special case and did not relish the status of qualifier, a role he soon abandoned. His promised return in 1983 did not materialise and he admitted he no longer had the desire to endure the relentless pressure involved in being the world's number one. Apart from being a widely respected figurehead for tennis, his competitive fire made him one of the wealthiest men in sport.

Jimmy Arias: tenacious.

Bjorn Borg: glittering triumphs.

The Stars/2

Pat Cash (Australia)
Pat Cash carries the hopes of Australia in that he is generally regarded as the best junior since John Newcombe to come out of that birthplace of tennis thoroughbreds. Born in Melbourne on 27 May 1965, he is 5ft 11in tall, powerfully built and looks much more mature than his years. He won the Wimbledon and US Open junior titles in 1982 and was runner-up in the French junior event. He seems to have the technique, physique and temperament to end Australia's search for another champion.

José-Luis Clerc (Argentina)
José-Luis Clerc is a player of highs and lows. The dashing Argentine won four Volvo Grand Prix 'super series' events in consecutive weeks in 1981, a year when he also won the Italian Open and reached the French semi-finals.

He was a key figure in his country's Davis Cup conquests of the United States in 1980 and 1983, beating John McEnroe on both occasions. But he ran into a trough in the middle of 1983, epitomised by a walk-off during a late-night doubles match in the Italian Open which led to him being defaulted in the singles where he was seeded second. Two Grand Prix wins in successive weeks, Boston and Washington, indicated he was pulling out of his slump.

Born in Buenos Aires on 16 August 1958, Clerc made a great recovery in 1975 when he sliced his left arm and leg in a fall from a hotel window in Dinard, France, which resulted in eight months' convalescence. He is coached by Pato Rodriguez, and married with one son.

Jimmy Connors (US)
Jimmy Connors reached another milestone in September 1983 when he won the US Open for the fifth time to record the 100th tournament victory of his

Pat Cash

José-Luis Clerc

Jimmy Connors

illustrious career. His success made him the first man in the game to win over $5m in prize money, and it came at the venerable tennis age of 31.

Connors seems to take the atmosphere of a prize fight on court with him and his willingness to give everything in pursuit of victory puts him among the most red-blooded competitors tennis has seen. He is a 100 per cent trier who could never be accused of not devoting maximum effort to every point.

He made a remarkable comeback in 1982, winning Wimbledon and the US Open at a time when many observers were ready to write him off as a candidate for the world's leading titles. His performance at Flushing Meadow in 1983 — when he destroyed Ivan Lendl in the final despite suffering from an injured toe and a stomach disorder — illustrated the fighting instinct of a player who thrives on pressure rather than being daunted by it.

Connors has won some magnificent matches and also provided the opposition when several players have enjoyed their finest moments — notably Arthur Ashe in the 1975 Wimbledon final, Manuel Orantes in the 1975 US Open and Guillermo Vilas in the US Open of 1977. His duels with Bjorn Borg will be remembered for their superior quality and impeccable sportsmanship.

His eagle-eyed return of service is the sharpest in the game, although his belligerent, two-handed backhand is another major weapon in his armoury. Behind the technique there is an uncrushable will to win, which is the most precious asset of this durable champion. He has created controversy in his years at the top but has never left a spectator feeling that he has not had value for money.

Connors was born on 2 September 1952 in Belleville, Illinois. His mother, Gloria, a teaching professional, was his greatest source of encouragement as a young man and Pancho Segura his most influential coach. All his natural talent and competitive spirit was suddenly converted into success in 1974 when he won the Wimbledon, US and Australian titles during a year when he lost only four matches.

The dominance of Borg in the late 1970s pushed Connors off his pinnacle and then McEnroe emerged to jostle for the world number one position, closely followed by Lendl. But for a decade Jimmy Connors was one of the hardest men in tennis to beat: Wimbledon champion in 1974 and 1982 and runner-up in 1975, 1977 and 1978; US champion in 1974, 1976, 1978, 1982 and 1983 and runner-up in 1975 and 1977; Grand Prix Masters champion in 1977 and 1980. The record speaks for itself.

Kevin Curren (South Africa)
Kevin Curren lost Wimbledon's finest match in 1983 — a five-set semi-final thriller against New Zealand's Chris Lewis — but he had a marvellous moment of glory in the fourth round when he defeated the defending champion, Jimmy Connors. The rangy, raw boned South African hit 33 aces past the finest returner of service in the world to achieve one of the great upsets of the tournament.

Curren was born in Durban on 2 March 1958 and was South Africa's junior champion before joining the University of Texas on a tennis scholarship. He turned professional after winning the National Collegiate Athletic Association singles title and soon became a circuit player no opponent could take lightly.

He has a successful doubles partnership with the Texan Steve Denton and they include the 1982 US Open title among their battle honours. Both

Steve Denton (left) and Kevin Curren

Curren and Denton have made steady improvement under the experienced eye of their travelling coach and mentor, Warren Jacques, a former Australian tournament player who is now based in Dallas.

Steve Denton (US)
They call Steve Denton 'The Bull' on the professional tour because of his height (6ft 2in), weight (190 pounds) and uncompromising aggression. Born at Kingsville, Texas, on 5 September 1956, Denton raced up the ratings list in 1981, moving from 409 on the computer at the beginning of the year to 24 at the end. His Australian coach, Warren Jacques, helped him to streamline his frame and his game. He formed a flourishing doubles combination with Kevin Curren and then began to pick off some celebrated singles rivals, including John McEnroe and Vitas Gerulaitis. A devastating server, he hit more aces than any other player in the 1982 Volvo Grand Prix.

Vitas Gerulaitis (US)
Vitas Gerulaitis keeps saying that he has had enough of the stress and training disciplines of life at the top of world tennis. However, he is a charismatic competitor whose speed of reflex and movement is a glittering asset. A taste for disco high life won him the title of 'Broadway Vitas' and he likes to mix and play with rock musicians.
   He was born on 26 July 1954 in New York where his father is the head

The Stars/4

teaching professional at the National Tennis Centre at Flushing Meadow. Vitas has been a consistent member of the world's top 10 since 1977, when he lost a memorable Wimbledon semi-final to his close friend Bjorn Borg.

José Higueras (Spain)
José Higueras has had to overcome a variety of obstacles to become one of the finest clay court players in the world. He started on the lowest rung of the tennis ladder as a ball boy at an expensive club in Granada, Spain. All his career he has suffered from insomnia, and in 1980 he contracted a lingering case of hepatitis.

In 1978 he walked off court in his Italian semi-final against Adriano Panatta in protest against crowd behaviour. But in the 1982 German final he stayed on court five hours and six minutes to beat Peter McNamara. He has won the British hard court title twice, in 1978 and 1983. He and his wife, Donna, have homes in Barcelona and Palm Springs.

Brian Gottfried (US)
When he was placed in the United States top 10 for the 10th time time in 11 years in 1983, Brian Gottfried became one of a group of only 20 players with similar credentials since the rankings were started in 1885. That in itself testified to the durability as well as the talent of this popular Baltimore player who was born on 27 January 1952.

Although the major titles have eluded him — he was runner-up in the French Open in 1977 and a Wimbledon semi-finalist in 1980 — Brian's career earnings of nearly $3m emphasise his match-winning ability. Gottfried and Raúl Ramírez have been one of the dominant doubles pairs of the Open era, winning one Wimbledon title, two French and four Italian.

Brian Gottfried: durable.

Johan Kriek (US)
Johan Kriek was a rugby half-back as a schoolboy and he brings something of the adroitness that position requires to his play, combining speed with a fiercely competitive attitude.

Born in Pongola, South Africa, on 5 April 1958 he went to the United States after first living in Vienna and became an American citizen in August 1982. He ended a period when he seemed fated to become one of the nearly-men of tennis by winning the Australian Open in 1981 and retaining the title the following year. Kriek lives in Naples, Florida, with his wife Tish and has earned $1m in prize money.

Henri Leconte (France)
Henri Leconte claimed two of the most celebrated scalps in tennis within two months in 1983. First the jaunty and purposeful Frenchman beat Bjorn Borg in the last competitive match of the mystic Swede's career at Monte

Johan Kriek: quick and adroit.

Carlo in March. Then in May he overwhelmed Ivan Lendl, the world's number one player at the time, in the WCT's Tournament of Champions at Forest Hills, New York.

Both performances illustrated the tremendous potential of the aggressive left hander from Lillers, who was born on 4 July 1963. Inconsistency is his greatest enemy but the guidance of a shrewd coach, Ion Tiriac, should help to erase this flaw in an otherwise intimidating game.

Ivan Lendl (Czechoslovakia)
Ivan Lendl has yet to win a major tournament after losing to Jimmy Connors for the second successive year in the final of the 1983 US Open. He is wealthy, having won well over $4m in prize money. He is also extremely talented: his forehand is the most ferocious stroke on the circuit and watching him detonate the shot is one of the more explosive sights in the game.

Despite the money and the technique, his sideboard has yet to be decorated with a Grand Slam trophy. The grave and inscrutable Czech has been in three major finals and lost them all. Bjorn Borg was his conqueror in the 1981 French Open and Connors beat him in the US Open in 1982 and 1983.

The best he has achieved at Wimbledon was to reach the 1983 semi-finals where he was defeated by John McEnroe. Although he is young enough to correct this imbalance in his career, it is clear that his main priority is to remove the mental blockage which seems to inhibit his performances in the events which matter most in terms of prestige and posterity.

Lendl is 6ft 2in tall — a thrilling and powerful player when he is able to win on his own terms. Yet he seems to lack the flexibility of shot to cope with an opponent who is able to absorb his aggression and dent the confidence which is vital to his game.

Ruthless, remorseless and humourless are words which leap to mind in describing him, but Ivan is not all that terrible off court. There is humour behind the mask he presents to the world at large and also a love of the good things of life. Although he gives 20 per cent of his earnings to the Czech Government he enjoys a comfortable living.

He has a house in Greenwich, Connecticut, and a place in Boca West, Florida. He owns a silver Mercedes and gold Porsche, but he continues to pursue the accolade which money cannot buy: a Grand Slam title.

Lendl was born in Ostrava on 7 March 1960. He may have inherited his dour demeanour from his father, Jiri, a lawyer who was once a ranked tennis player in Czechoslovakia and is now an accomplished exponent of chess. His mother, Olga, was once second in the Czech tennis rankings.

He was the world's top junior in

The Stars/5

1978 and his career since then has been one of steady and lucrative progress. His mentor is the Polish player, Wojtek Fibak. Off-court he has an obsessive enthusiasm for golf.

At tennis press conferences — for which he has a well-known antipathy — he revels in the laconic reply to reporters' questions. 'What happened, Ivan?' asked one journalist after a victory which apparently needed interpreting. 'I won,' said Ivan, who makes the late Gary Cooper seem like a chatterbox.

Chris Lewis (New Zealand)

Chris Lewis won the most stirring match of the 1983 Wimbledon championships when he defeated the South African Kevin Curren 6–7 6–4 7–6 6–7 8–6 to become the first unseeded finalist in the men's singles for 16 years. He was ranked 91 in the world at the time and his achievement in becoming the first New Zealander to reach the final since Tony Wilding played in the 1914 Challenge Round inspired nearly 1,000 good luck messages. John McEnroe outclassed him in the final but the athletic and agile Lewis had left a memorable imprint on the tournament.

Born on 9 March 1957 in Auckland, he began playing at the age of 6, encouraged by his tennis-playing father. He was the world's top junior in 1975. Chris runs and practises for up to six hours a day to keep himself at peak fitness. A narrow escape in South America when a plane was forced into an emergency landing left him with a dislike of flying and he drives to tournaments whenever he can.

Gene Mayer (US)

Gene Mayer has kept his position among the world's leading players despite being unusually injury-prone. Born on 11 April 1956 in New York, he hits the ball two-handed on both sides with a rare command of touch and angle.

His older brother, Sandy, with whom he won the 1979 French doubles title, says that Gene has so many different types of game 'if one isn't working he throws it away and tries another'. Apart from his achievements on court, Gene's voracious appetite for food is legendary.

Retirements and scratchings because of injury mar his record. However, his two-fisted talents have earned him well over $1m since he graduated from Stanford University.

Tim Mayotte (US)

A Wimbledon semi-finalist in 1982 and a quarter-finalist in 1981 and 1983, Tim Mayotte is the latest product of Stanford University to find success on the professional tour (the others include John McEnroe, Roscoe Tanner, Gene and Sandy Mayer and

Ivan Lendl (left); Gene Mayer (below)

Pat DuPre). He was born in Springfield, Massachusetts on 3 August 1960 and first came into prominence when he beat Jimmy Connors in the second round of the 1980 Transamerica Open. Sometimes known as 'Gentleman Tim' because of his genial disposition, he is the youngest of eight children. His brother, Chris, is also on the tour.

John McEnroe (US)

John McEnroe's insistence that he wants to be remembered for his tennis not his temper seemed to be gaining substance at Wimbledon in 1983 when he recaptured the men's title with a performance in the final which was almost angelic in its benevolence. After devastating the unseeded Chris Lewis 6–2 6–2 6–2 in an incident-free contest which was the quickest men's final of the Open era, he kissed the Challenge Cup and shook hands with every official within reach.

A new McEnroe? His British audience can only wait and see but spectators obviously found it pleasing to applaud a performance which revealed the sublime rather than the darker side of his complex character. If he does succeed in controlling the most volcanic temperament in sport it will mean the end of a glossary of unflattering press descriptions, from the overplayed 'Superbrat' to 'Mac the Strife', the 'Prince of Petulance' and the 'Merchant of Menace'.

McEnroe's attitude to umpires and linesmen soon became well defined after his dramatic breakthrough in 1977, when he reached the Wimbledon semi-finals as an 18-year-old qualifier. He demands from officials the same perfection he expects of himself. When he does not get it — and calling the lines in top tennis is the hardest job in sport — he erupts, firm in the belief that he is correct after playing the game since the age of eight and being blessed with sensitivity of vision.

The fact that he is not always right has not deterred McEnroe one iota. He has a strong sense of justice, particularly when it relates to himself, and he is also keenly aware of the fine line which separates victory from defeat in the upper echelons of the game. McEnroe admits that he is partially to blame for all the fuss he creates but he has persisted in pandering to the devil which ignites his Irish temper.

If it is possible to detach the shots from the behaviour you are left with a player of rare ability, a master improviser who can wriggle out of the tightest of corners, a sorcerer in terms of racket control and a demon when it comes to delivering his left-handed serve. In other words he is a very fine tennis player — and he is often willing to play for his country in the Davis Cup.

McEnroe was born on 16 February 1959 in Wiesbaden, West Germany, where his father — now a Wall Street lawyer in charge of his son's business affairs — was serving at an American Air Force base. He grew up in Douglaston, New York, and became a student at Stanford University where he returned after his Wimbledon run of 1977 to win the National Collegiate singles title.

His career as a professional has been sprinkled with brilliant matches, including the unforgettable 1980 Wimbledon final against Borg which the Swede won 1–6 7–5 6–3 6–7 8–6 after McEnroe had captured the fourth set on a tie-break of 34 points. McEnroe went on to prove his class by beating Borg in the US final in the same year and repeating the process at Wimbledon and Flushing Meadow in 1981 — the latter victory making him the first American to win the US title three successive times since Bill Tilden in the 1920s.

John McEnroe: mercurial maestro.

The Stars/7

Connors snatched his Wimbledon crown away from him in 1982, but after an injury-plagued start to 1983 McEnroe peaked perfectly to regain the title in July. London has proved to be a profitable source of inspiration for McEnroe. His Wimbledon triumph was his ninth singles title there — two Wimbledons, four Benson and Hedges at Wembley and three Stella Artois at Queen's. An avid rock fan, McEnroe plays the guitar and has appeared on stage with several bands.

Buster Mottram (GB)

Buster Mottram's growing disenchantment with Grand Prix tennis led him to announce in September 1983 that he would no longer be competing on the circuit. The British number one, tired of the pressure of pursuing computer points, said he would confine his activities to team competitions, British tournaments, the German League — where he represents a club — and possibly the occasional WCT event.

The news did not come as a surprise after a disappointing year when his world ranking slumped and he talked about his ambitions to enter politics as a Conservative candidate. A stubborn competitor who was ranked 19th in the world in 1982, Buster (whose first name is Christopher) never showed the drive to break into the top 10.

He intends to retain his commitment to the Davis Cup where he has made a formidable spearhead for the British team — notably in the epic run to the final against the United States at Palm Springs in 1978 where he beat Brian Gottfried from match point down to record Britain's only victory in a 4–1 defeat. He was born at Wimbledon on 25 April 1955, the son of Tony Mottram, a former British number one (1946–55), and Joy Gannon, who played for Britain in the Wightman Cup.

Yannick Noah (France)

The summer of 1983 was a mixture of joy and dismay for Yannick Noah, the black Frenchman with the Rastafarian dreadlocks who was discovered in the French Cameroons by Arthur Ashe in 1971. Noah became the first French player to win the French Open for 37 years when he beat Sweden's Mats Wilander in the final.

In the same year he was also suspended for 84 days by the Men's International Professional Tennis Council for failing to appear in a round robin event in the World Team Cup. An adventurous player with a flamboyant style, Noah was born on 16 May 1960. He is at the heart of the French tennis revival and led his country's team to the 1982 Davis Cup final against the United States at Grenoble where he lost to John McEnroe in five sets.

Guillermo Vilas (Argentina)

A shadow fell over the career of Guillermo Vilas in the middle of 1983 when he was suspended for a year by the Men's International Professional Tennis Council for allegedly accepting guaranteed appearance money at the Rotterdam Grand Prix tournament. Vilas appealed and other top players criticised the harshness of the sentence.

The Argentine left-hander, who celebrated his 31st birthday on 17 August 1983, broke through in 1974 when he won the Masters on grass at Melbourne and went on to consolidate his position in the world's top 10. He enjoyed a particularly successful year in 1977 when he captured the French and US Open titles. He won the Australian Open in 1978 and 1979 and the Italian title in 1980, and his achievements helped to inspire a resurgence of interest in tennis in South America.

Vilas is a poet with two published volumes of his work. He became head-

Yannick Noah (above): experienced joy and dismay in 1983, when he won the French Open and was also suspended.

Buster Mottram (left): stubborn competitor, who has quit the Grand Prix circuit.

The Stars/8

line material on newspaper gossip pages for a well-publicised friendship with Princess Caroline of Monaco.

Mats Wilander (Sweden)
Only one thing ruffles the imperturbable Mats Wilander and that is to be compared with Bjorn Borg. The similarities are obvious — Mats is Swedish, fair-haired, hits a double-handed backhand and has Bjorn's rigid concentration — but understandably he prefers to be his own man: the first Wilander as opposed to the second Borg.

Born in the small industrial town of Vaxjo on 22 May 1964, Wilander began playing on a parking lot at the age of six, became a leading Swedish junior and won the French junior title in 1981. He returned to Stade Roland Garros in 1982 to capture the French Open at the age of 17 years, 9 months and 6 days — the youngest player ever to win one of the Grand Slam tournaments. To emphasise that this triumph was not a fluke he collected three other Grand Prix titles before the end of a year when it was clear that a new star had arrived in the tennis firmament.

Women

Tracy Austin (US)
Back and shoulder injuries have dogged Tracy Austin in recent years but she remains a household name: a phenomenon who was a veteran before she was 20 and has never been outside the world's top 25 since making her debut on the computer in July 1977. Born on 12 December 1962 at Rolling Hills, California, Tracy had earned $1m from tennis by August 1980. Her total of 25 American junior titles is a record.

In January 1977 she became the youngest player to capture a profes-

Mats Wilander (top) and Tracy Austin.

sional singles title when she won the Avon Futures of Portland. Two years later her precocious skills made her the youngest ever US Open champion at the age of 16 years 9 months.

Tracy is a member of a tennis-playing family which produced three national junior champions in addition to herself. John and Tracy Austin are the only brother-sister team to win the Wimbledon mixed doubles — a feat they achieved in 1980.

Carling Bassett (Canada)
Carling Bassett, a Toronto teenager who is 'Darling Carling' to Canadian tennis enthusiasts, proved that she had talent besides good looks and wealthy parents by reaching the last 16 at Wimbledon in 1983. She was born on 9 October 1967 and came to prominence in 12-and-under events.

Her father is a former Canadian Davis Cup player who has owned Montreal Canadiens and the Toronto Maple Leafs in the National (Ice) Hockey League, plus the Memphis franchise in the World Football League. He produced a tennis film called *Sneakers* starring Carling, whose name relates to her mother's family — the founders of a well-known brewery.

Bettina Bunge (West Germany)
Bettina Bunge was born in Switzerland of German parents on 13 June 1963, lived for 13 years in Peru — where she won the national title aged 13 — moved to Florida and rents an apartment in Monte Carlo. She represents West Germany in the Federation Cup but travels on a US visa as a resident alien.

From this cosmopolitan background has emerged a formidable player whose biggest fault is inconsistency. Bettina entered the top 10 in 1981 and, despite a few erratic streaks, has consolidated her position with performances underlining her exceptional talent.

Jo Durie (GB)
Jo Durie looks six feet tall but insists

Jo Durie: steady improvement.

defiantly that her height is 5ft 11½in. Whatever the vital statistics, she is a big girl with the kind of physique to withstand the rigours of the women's circuit.

Her rise to becoming Britain's number one almost ended before it began in 1980 when she underwent a critical spinal operation which kept her off court for eight months. She returned with a winning streak of fifteen matches and has maintained a steady improvement, guided by her coach Alan Jones.

Born in Bristol on 27 July 1960, she gave a welcome fillip to British tennis in 1983 by reaching the semi-finals of the French Open and the US Open. It was a magnificent achievement, but she shares her coach's belief that the best is yet to come.

Zina Garrison (US)
Zina Garrison, a product of the public parks in Houston, Texas, is one of the game's outstanding prospects. Born on

The Stars/9

16 November 1963, the youngest in a family of seven children, she began playing tennis at the age of 10 and subsequently became the first black girl to be ranked number one in Texas.

In 1981 she received the International Tennis Federation's Junior of the Year award after winning the junior titles at Wimbledon and the US Open. Bold, adventurous and mobile she has the ability to please crowds as well as win matches.

Andrea Jaeger (US)
Andrea Jaeger was outplayed 6–0 6–3 by Martina Navratilova when she reached her first Wimbledon final in 1983 but youth is on her side as she continues to pursue the game's major prizes. Born on 4 June 1965 in Chicago, Illinois, she made a sensational start to her professional career in 1980 by winning thirteen successive matches from pre-qualifying onwards to take the Avon Futures title at Las Vegas.

By the end of the year she was one of the top seven women in the world after a dramatic surge to prominence which surprised even her ex-boxer father and coach, Roland. Since then Andrea has settled down at number three behind Miss Navratilova and Chris Lloyd. She is a shrewd strategist who has won over $1m in three seasons.

Billie Jean King (US)
Billie Jean King gambolled through Wimbledon in 1983 with a zest which mocked the fact that she was in her 40th year. She became the tournament's oldest women's semi-finalist since Mrs Lambert Chambers reached the Challenge Round in 1920, aged 41.

Andrea Jaeger ended her run, and defeat in the mixed doubles final meant that Billie Jean was unable to add another Wimbledon title to her record total of 20 (6 singles, 10 doubles, 4 mixed). But once again she had left a memorable imprint on an event which has been the scene of

Zina Garrison: adventurous.

Andrea Jaeger: shrewd.

some of the greatest triumphs of a distinguished career.

Born on 22 November 1943 in Long Beach, California, Mrs King is the only woman to win US singles titles on all four surfaces — grass, indoor, clay and hard courts. Her achievements were interspersed with three knee operations and ankle surgery.

A fervent advocate of the women's game and women's sport in general, she enjoyed worldwide coverage when she beat Bobby Riggs, a former US men's champion, in a challenge match at Houston Astrodome in 1973. Off-court she is involved in a number of publishing and promotion enterprises with her husband, Larry King.

Chris Lloyd (US)

Wimbledon saw the end of an astonishing record in 1983 when Chris Lloyd was beaten in the third round by a fellow American, Kathy Jordan. It was the first time Mrs Lloyd had been defeated before the semi-final round in the 34 Grand Slam tournaments in which she had played since 1971. This amazing run underlined the consistency of a champion whose competitive skills have always been allied to grace and charm.

Her rigid concentration and metronomic efficiency from the baseline earned her the title of 'Ice Maiden' when she first surfaced in the big time as a 16-year-old semi-finalist in the 1971 US Open. Subsequently the public warmed to a sporting competitor who rejected more than $50,000 in prize money to remain an amateur until her 18th birthday.

Her achievements make her one of the great players in the modern game: Wimbledon champion in 1974, 1976 and 1981; US Open champion in 1975, 1976, 1977, 1978, 1980 and 1982; French champion in 1974, 1975, 1979, 1980 and 1983; Australian champion in 1982. Fifteen Grand Slam singles titles, but never the Grand Slam itself although she went to Wimbledon in 1983 as holder of the US, French and Australian championships (where she had beaten Martina Navratilova in three sets on grass).

Chris is unbeaten in Wightman Cup singles (22 victories) and also in the Federation Cup (28). Her 56 match-winning streak in 1974 is a women's record and she also holds the record for most consecutive victories on one surface: 125 on clay from August 1973 to May 1979. She was born on 21 December 1954 at Fort Lauderdale, Florida where her father, Jim, is a teaching professional. She married the British Davis Cup player, John Lloyd, on 17 April 1979.

The Stars/10

Chris Lloyd: grace and charm.

Martina Navratilova and (inset) Hana Mandlikova.

The Stars/11

Hana Mandlikova (Czechoslovakia)
Few women players can combine grace and aggression so endearingly as Hana Mandlikova. This stylish Czech won the French Open in 1981, the Australian title in 1980 and has been runner-up at Wimbledon (1981) and the US Open (1980). Her rise to the top was relentless — from the International Tennis Federation's world junior champion in 1978 to the Women's Tennis Association's 'most impressive newcomer' in 1979 and the tour's 'most improved player' in 1980.

If her game seemed to have reached a plateau in 1983 her youth — she was born on 19 February 1962 — suggests that there is ample time for Hana's flair to carry her to new heights. With so little margin for error in her approach she will always be prone to unexpected disaster but class will surely reap its just reward.

Martina Navratilova (US)
Martina Navratilova conceded only twenty-five games in seven matches to win the Wimbledon singles title in 1983 for the second successive year and fourth time in all. That put her half way towards the record of eight established by Helen Wills Moody between 1927 and 1938, and few observers could question her ability to go on and surpass it, even in the harsher competition of the modern era.

Ted Tinling, who has no peer as an authority on women's tennis, believes that Martina is close to becoming the greatest woman competitor the game has seen, even greater than his lifelong idol Suzanne Lenglen. Backed by a team of advisers including a coach, a nutritionist and a motivator she certainly looks the complete player: a 'bionic wonder woman' whose only flaw could be something a computer cannot handle — a frailty of temperament which can lead to unexpected setbacks such as her defeat by

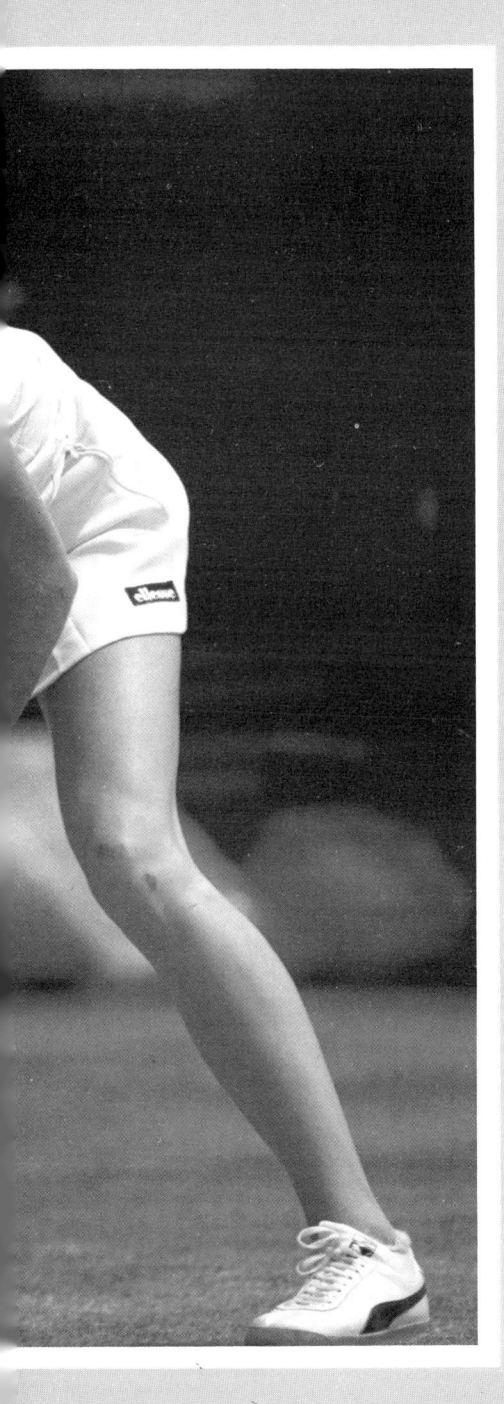

Kathy Horvath in the 1983 French Open.

Martina was born on 18 October 1956 in Prague, Czechoslovakia, but defected to the United States in September 1975 and became a US citizen in July 1981. She captured the Australian Open in 1981, the French Open in 1982 and followed her 1983 Wimbledon triumph by winning the US Open for the first time — conceding only nineteen games in seven matches.

She was the first tennis professional to pass the $4m mark in prize money, and the first woman player to earn over $1m in a single year — 1982, when she won 15 out of 18 tournaments and 90 out of 93 matches.

Pam Shriver (US)
Pam Shriver set two records in her breakthrough year of 1978. The lanky Marylander was the first player to come through pre-qualifying, qualifying and main draw to capture an Avon Futures event, winning twelve consecutive matches. Then she became the youngest women's finalist in US Open history at the age of 16 years 2 months.

Subsequently she developed a worrying shoulder problem which called for a special weight-training programme, but her forthright serve and volley have kept her in the forefront of the women's game. She shares a powerful doubles partnership with Martina Navratilova and their haul of titles includes a Wimbledon hat trick, 1981–2–3.

Andrea Temesvari (Hungary)
Andrea Temesvari is the most gifted woman to emerge from Eastern Europe since Czechoslovakia's Hana Mandlikova. Born in Budapest on 26 April 1966 she made her first impact on the women's tour in 1981 when she

Andrea Temesvari: gifted Hungarian.

The Stars/12

reached the Nice final and came within two points of beating Andrea Jaeger in the French Open.

She won her first major event in 1983 when she captured the Italian title. Andrea is coached by her father, Otto, a former Olympic basketball player who decided that the best way for her to succeed in the women's game was to play like a man.

Virginia Wade: Wimbledon tightrope.

Wendy Turnbull (Australia)
Wendy Turnbull is best known to the British public as the nimble Australian girl who partnered John Lloyd to a rare British success at Wimbledon in the 1983 mixed doubles. But apart from helping Lloyd to become the first British man to win a Wimbledon title since Fred Perry in 1936, Wendy is one of the most consistent and successful players in women's tennis.

A native of Brisbane where she was born on 26 November 1952, Wendy was not a junior star but improved rapidly once she began her career in the senior game. Called 'Rabbit' because of her fleet-footed agility, she has been in the world's top 10 since 1977, when she was runner-up in the US Open.

Virginia Wade (GB)
Revitalised by the elixir which only Wimbledon can distil, Virginia Wade surprised everyone, including herself, by reaching the last eight of the singles in 1983 with a harum-scarum mixture of brilliance and good fortune. Although her summer escapade was ended by South Africa's Yvonne Vermaak it was a remarkable feat by a 37-year-old veteran who exhibited a teenager's vitality as she wrote another vivid chapter in her personal Wimbledon story.

Walking the Wimbledon tightrope with Virginia became a national pastime for the British public in the 1960s and 1970s and there was jubilation when she won the title with exquisite timing in 1977, the tournament's centenary year. Miss Wade, who says she now 'plays for fun', also won the US (1968), Italian (1971) and Australian (1972) titles in a career where she earned well over $1m in tournament competition.

She is a tennis commentator on British and American TV and in 1982 became the first woman to be elected to the committee of the All England Club. Born in Bournemouth on 10 July 1945, she grew up in South Africa where her father was an Episcopal Archdeacon. She now lives in New York City.

Road to the top

British tennis took a significant step towards the modern way of rearing champions in September 1983 when four boys became the first juniors in the country to combine their normal education with specialist tennis tuition. The boys — Colin Beecher, aged 12, from Hayes, Kent; David Harris, 12, from Chingford, Essex; Ulrich Nganga, 13, from Norwich, Norfolk, and Nicholas Smith, 12, from Blundellsands, Lancashire — attend schools in Buckinghamshire close to the National Training Centre at Bisham Abbey.

Similar schemes had already been established in Europe — notably France — and the Lawn Tennis Association hoped that the combination of study and play would help to reduce the gap between the standard of British juniors and their European and American counterparts.

It was intended to expand the project and Paul Hutchins, the British team manager, said: 'With world junior standards being so high and our normal education system not allowing many of our good prospects the chance to combine tennis with their education, we hope this plan will go some way to at least giving certain youngsters an opportunity to fulfil their potential.'

After the arrival of Open tennis and the prize money explosion which followed, it soon became clear that a new era in the game would be accompanied by a fresh approach to the development of future champions. As competition sharpened, the road to the top became more arduous.

The United States college system continues to provide a flood of talented men and women. France, Sweden, West Germany and Czechoslovakia have moved with the times in terms of nurturing fledgling talent. Britain has fallen behind nations who are producing champions.

Every country has its lean spells and Britain is in the throes of a tennis drought. Champions are born not manufactured but, meanwhile, the LTA is working towards a structure which will give the embryonic star a chance to shine from an early age.

Short tennis is an important feature of the LTA's relentless search for promising players. This is a miniature version of tennis played on a court the size of that used for badminton, using a plastic racket and yellow foam balls with a slow flight and a consistent bounce. The game removes all the difficulties of playing tennis for youngsters under 10 — big court,

Short tennis

heavy racket, fast, high bouncing balls — while retaining the basic ingredients of lawn tennis. Children learn to rally and develop an appetite for playing which they will retain as they grow older.

The LTA has taken short tennis into primary and middle schools, clubs, sports centres and village halls all over the country and has organised county and regional tournaments. It remains to be seen whether a praiseworthy attempt to bring tennis within the reach of small children achieves the desired results.

Apart from short tennis, 35,000 children a year are involved in the LTA Prudential Grass Roots scheme for beginners. This leads to outstanding prospects being selected for special training, which opens the door to county junior squads, regional squads and, for the most gifted, training at national level at Bisham Abbey.

Most children who are drawn to tennis come from tennis backgrounds in that their parents usually play the game. How far a youngster's ambition takes him depends not only on talent but determination to climb the long ladder from aspiring newcomer in a local tournament to Grand Prix competitor.

Equipment

Leading players invariably link their tournament achievements to a handsome income from endorsing a wide range of products. One of the most highly publicised deals of recent years was a reported $3m five-year agreement between John McEnroe and Dunlop, the sporting goods manufacturers.

But the player with the true Midas touch was Bjorn Borg. Commercial

Bjorn Borg: Midas touch has brought a string of endorsements.

John McEnroe: million-dollar deal.

endorsements by a player reached unparalleled heights when Borg was enjoying the phenomenal run of success which saw him win five successive Wimbledon titles and take the French Open six times.

Borg became a hot commercial property not only on the court where every item of equipment he used represented an endorsement — from his wrist and head bands to the strings in his racket — but off it where he lent his name to merchandise as varied as clogs, jeans and a sewing machine, to jigsaws, toys and soft drinks. Even in retirement his name retains a charismatic appeal to advertisers.

The money spent on endorsements reflects the astonishing expansion in the range of tennis goods following the arrival of Open tennis. What was once a relatively small corner of the sporting market is now a huge industry, offering a variety of choice undreamt of before the floodgates of commercialism were thrown open.

Faced with so many alternatives in rackets, footwear and clothing — many of which are accompanied by the unqualified support of some of the best-known exponents of the game — the average player can be left in a state of quivering indecision. A good rule-of-thumb judgement is to go for what feels right — without risking an overdraft. The most expensive racket in the shop will not make a weekend player a champion overnight — any more than the costly shoes, shirts and shorts which carry the blessing of some photogenic celebrity.

The most significant trend in rackets in recent years has been the swing away from the conventional head size (70 sq in) to the oversize (100 sq in) and mid-size (85 sq in) whose virtues are a larger hitting area and more power. Apart from the traditional wood, rackets are now made from metal, fibre-glass, graphite and various composites. They all have their advantages. But club players should let comfort — and realism — be their guide.

Technique

Forehand
Hit from the same side as the hand holding the racket. Most players use the Eastern grip, although there are variations called Western and Continental. The Eastern is also known as the 'shake hands' grip because the player is virtually shaking hands with the racket handle. The first shot taught by coaches, the forehand should be struck with the racket parallel with the ground.

Backhand
Hit from the opposite side to the hand holding the racket, the backhand is the bane of many club players who approach the shot with more apprehension than the forehand. Tennis has bred some legendary backhands: Don Budge, Ken Rosewall, Rod Laver and Arthur Ashe; Bjorn Borg, Jimmy Connors and Chris Lloyd with their two-handers.

Backhand: Arthur Ashe.

Service
The only stroke in tennis over which the player has complete control comes in three variations: flat, slice and kick. It is arguably the most important shot of all because it starts and sets the tone of rallies. If a player is serving well it gives a fillip to the rest of his game.

Volley
Struck before the ball has had time to bounce, the volley is the most positive way of gaining the initiative and ending a rally. Sometimes the incoming volleyer is caught at his feet and is forced to return the ball immediately after it has bounced. This is known as a half-volley.

Lob
The simplest and most effective shot in tennis is basically a drive with a lifted follow through up and under the ball. In this way the ball is hoisted

Serve: Pam Shriver.

Volley: Billie Jean King.

over an opponent's head, giving the lobber time to gather his wits and resources.

Smash

Performed with a service action, the smash is the definitive answer to the lob and the most spectacular shot in the armoury of tennis. Most top players are good overhead because if they did not have a reliable smash they would be lobbed remorselessly.

Smash executed by Chris Lewis.

Events and competitions

The Grand Prix is the major international men's professional tennis circuit. In 1983 it linked 81 tournaments in 26 countries on 6 continents. These included the Grand Slam events — Wimbledon, US, French and Australian Opens — in a total of 21 national championships.

Since the birth of the Grand Prix in 1970 prize money has increased by 560 per cent. In 1983 it was $15m, plus $3m in a bonus pool. The bonus pool offers $600,000 to the year's leading singles player and $150,000 to the player with the most points earned in doubles. It is shared by the top 32 singles players and the top 16 doubles players.

The Masters is the annual finale to the circuit, involving the twelve players who lead the Grand Prix points standings at the end of the year. The tournament was held in a different country in each of its first seven years but from 1977 it has made New York's Madison Square Garden a permanent home.

The Grand Slam, which means being the current holder of all four major singles titles, is the most elusive feat in the game and has been achieved by only four players — Don Budge (1938), Rod Laver (1962 and 1969), Maureen Connolly (1953) and Margaret Court (1970). As standards rise it is becoming progressively harder to exert the dominance needed to be the world's best on grass (Wimbledon and Australia), clay (French) and rubberised asphalt (US).

Despite the antipathy of some players towards grass — a surface which has become a comparative rarity as tennis has moved away from the original concept of a game to be played on lawns — Wimbledon remains the world's premier tournament, where a title means a place in tennis history.

Wimbledon is the Everest of tennis and nobody would belittle the problems of climbing that particular summit. But the most exacting test in the game is the French Open where the rallies are much longer than the abbreviated exchanges produced by grass, and only the fittest survive.

Two firmly established British events in the Grand Prix are the Stella Artois grass court championships at

Queen's Club, London — an important part in players' preparations for Wimbledon — and the Benson and Hedges championships at Wembley in November — a particularly rewarding hunting ground for John McEnroe.

The Virginia Slims World Championship Series is a year-round women's circuit embracing 4 continents and 11 countries with indoor and outdoor competition on 4 different surfaces (clay, cement, grass and carpet). It offers more than $11m in prize money, and a $1m bonus pool is shared by the 40 singles players and 20 doubles players with the highest points standings.

Queen's Club: setting for a Wimbledon warm-up event.

Events and competitions/2

World Championship Tennis, the Dallas-based promoters, filed an antitrust lawsuit against the Men's International Professional Tennis Council, the International Tennis Federation and the Association of Tennis Professionals. However, in November 1983, they agreed to toe the Grand Prix line for five years, starting in 1985. The lawsuit was also dropped.

WCT put nearly $10m in prize money into their 22-event 1982 circuit and another $3.7m in 1983. The 1984 WCT schedule takes in the Barratt World Doubles at the Royal Albert Hall, London, Richmond, Houston, the WCT finals in Dallas and the Tournament of Champions at Forest Hills.

There are four major international team competitions: the Davis Cup, the Federation Cup, the Wightman Cup and the King's Cup.

The Davis Cup, the men's international team championship, was born in Boston, Massachusetts, in 1900 when the United States beat Great Britain 3–0. The name is drawn from that of its American instigator, the late Dwight Davis (1879–1945) who commissioned a silver punch bowl and offered it for international competition.

At first only Britain and America entered but other nations soon showed interest and the championship became one of the world's great team events. The Challenge Round system, in which the champion nation was required to play only the title match, was abolished in 1972.

The Federation Cup, the international team championship for women, was launched in 1963, a year which marked the fiftieth anniversary of the International Lawn Tennis Federation. Unlike the Davis Cup it is completed in a week. Each tie is composed of two singles and a doubles. The first event was held at Queen's Club, London, and since then it has been staged at different venues in many parts of the world.

The Wightman Cup is an annual contest between the women of Britain and the United States played alternately in the two countries. It is named after the American donor of the trophy, the late Hazel Hotchkiss Wightman (1886–1974). The first tie was held in 1923 and the format remains the same: five singles and two doubles.

The King's Cup is an indoor team competition for European nations. It was named after the donor, King Gustav V of Sweden, a tennis enthusiast. Matches comprise two singles and a doubles.

Grand Slam: Rod Laver.

Grand Slam: Margaret Court.

Venues

At the Stade Roland Garros, where the French championships are staged, the playing surface is clay and the game becomes a searching test of ability, patience and endurance. With each men's match the best of five sets, there is no short cut to the title.

Roland Garros reflects the health and prosperity of tennis in France. The stadium has had a face-lift which shows that even tennis arenas can be chic. Led by its progressive chairman, Philippe Chatrier, the tournament is now in the game's forefront as it sets the pace in prize money and slick administration.

American tennis moved into a new era in 1978 with the opening of the National Tennis Centre at Flushing Meadow, New York — the successor to Forest Hills as the home of the US Open. Forest Hills, with its horseshoe-shaped stadium and Tudor club house, was outgrown by a booming game although it remains the venue for WCT's Tournament of Champions.

Flushing Meadow was described as a marshland dump in Scott Fitzgerald's novel *The Great Gatsby* but it became the home of the World Fair in 1939 and 1964 and a temporary base for the United Nations. The rebuilt stadium was originally named after the jazz giant Louis Armstrong whose widow Lucille attended the opening ceremony.

The venue is brash, usually sweltering and invariably noisy — apart from the crowd it is on the flight path to La Guardia airport — but it has taken the Open away from a club atmosphere to the public at large with an annual attendance of over 350,000.

In 1982, a rejuvenated Australian Open had the strongest field assembled for the event since Open tennis arrived in 1968. It was also the first single Australian sporting event to carry prize money of over $1m. The tournament is played in the spectacular Kooyong Stadium in Melbourne — a bastion of grass court tennis where

Flushing Meadow: brash and noisy.

Plan of Wimbledon

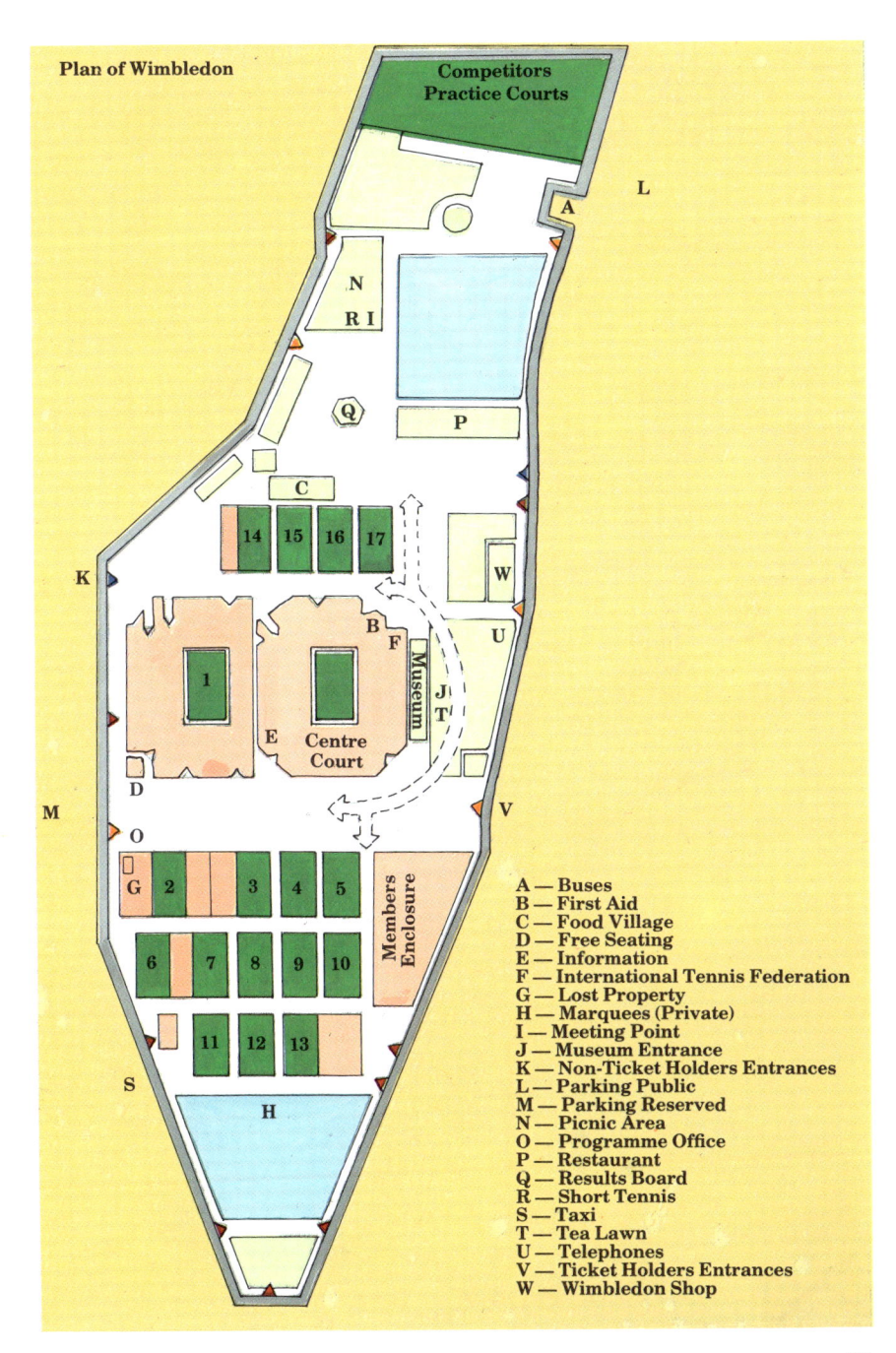

A — Buses
B — First Aid
C — Food Village
D — Free Seating
E — Information
F — International Tennis Federation
G — Lost Property
H — Marquees (Private)
I — Meeting Point
J — Museum Entrance
K — Non-Ticket Holders Entrances
L — Parking Public
M — Parking Reserved
N — Picnic Area
O — Programme Office
P — Restaurant
Q — Results Board
R — Short Tennis
S — Taxi
T — Tea Lawn
U — Telephones
V — Ticket Holders Entrances
W — Wimbledon Shop

53

many great Australian players made their first impact on the world game.

Wimbledon and the world

Wimbledon is a celebration as much as a championship — an annual gathering of tennis players and lovers of the game where history is made on the lawns which serve as a stage.

It is strawberries and cream, scurrying ball boys, the Royal Box, sky-high winners and sad-eyed losers. It is London at the height of the summer; Dan Maskell telling a breathless television audience that this is set, match or championship point; the covers going on and the covers coming off.

Wimbledon might be only one of many big money events in these bonanza days for tournament competitors. But its place at the centre of tennis is secure. No other tournament has its prestige or pulling power.

The first genuine stars of Wimbledon were the twin brothers William and Ernest Renshaw, from Cheltenham. Their genius for bold and aggressive play opened up new horizons for lawn tennis as a spectacular sport.

William Renshaw was singles champion seven times between 1881 and 1889, which remains a men's record. That was in the days of the Challenge Round, where the title-holder waited for the best of his rivals to emerge.

Ernest Renshaw won the Wimbledon singles in 1888. A brilliant combination, the Renshaws took the doubles title for the fifth time in 1889 and then retired. Their record as a pair included seven years without defeat.

By 1891, with the decline of the Renshaws, Wimbledon's fortunes were sagging. It took two more brothers, Reggie and Laurie Doherty, to breathe new and lasting life into the championships between 1897 and 1906. The 'Prince Charmings' of lawn tennis, they did more than any other men to spread and popularise the game around the world.

If the Renshaws laid the seed of modern lawn tennis, the Dohertys brought it to full flower. Reggie won four Wimbledon singles titles. Laurie took the title five successive times before retiring in 1906 as unbeaten champion. As a doubles pair they won Wimbledon eight times.

At first the championships were for men only but a women's singles event was introduced in 1884 when Maud Watson beat her sister Lilian to become the first women's champion. This prepared the way for a teenage heroine, Lottie Dod, who won the first of her 5 titles in 1887 at the age of 15.

The rise of Suzanne Lenglen and Bill Tilden coincided with the All England Club's move from Worple Road to its present ground in Church Road, opened by King George V in 1922 when the challenge round was abolished. Mlle Lenglen, still regarded by some observers as the greatest woman player, won the title six times in seven years. Bill Tilden, another popular competitor who left an enormous imprint on the game, won his first Wimbledon aged 27 and his third and last at 37.

The 1920s amounted to a French takeover of Wimbledon. Suzanne Lenglen's achievements were supported in the men's singles by her compatriots Jean Borotra (champion in 1924 and 1926), René Lacoste (1925 and 1928) and Henri Cochet (1927 and 1929), with the doubles specialist Jacques Brugnon sharing in four doubles titles. Britain's dashing Fred Perry dominated the mid-1930s. He won the men's title in 1934, 1935 and 1936 and British tennis is still searching for a champion cast in the same mould.

Lew Hoad: great champion.

The United States cheered the poker-faced dominance of Helen Wills Moody, who won the women's title eight times between 1927 and 1938, and the impact of Don Budge, one of the most complete players the game has seen with a backhand of unsurpassed purity and penetration. Budge was the first man to win all three Wimbledon titles in one year, 1937. He repeated the feat in 1938, when he became the first winner of the Grand Slam by holding the world's four major titles — Australia, France, Wimbledon and the United States.

The Centre Court was damaged by bombs in the Second World War but peace saw the championships pick up where they left off, producing a string of great champions — Jack Kramer, Frank Sedgman, Lew Hoad, Rod Laver, Maureen Connolly, Margaret Court and Billie Jean King — as lawn tennis moved towards Open status.

The world's first Open tournament — with amateurs competing against professionals — was at Bournemouth in 1968. Although the amazingly durable Ken Rosewall beat Rod Laver in the final, it was Laver who won the first Open Wimbledon to become undisputed world champion.

Two Wimbledon titles as an amateur (1961–2) and two as a professional (1968–9) plus two Grand Slams (1962 and 1969) established Laver as a tennis immortal. The Australian left-hander with the technique for all surfaces dominated the 1960s.

The 1970s saw a tennis explosion among players and spectators. The growth in popularity was astonishing, and Wimbledon played an integral part in a changing era.

There was one historic squall. In 1973, Nikki Pilic (Yugoslavia) was suspended by the ITF because of his alleged refusal to play in the Davis Cup. Wimbledon would not accept Pilic's entry in view of the decision and the ATP called on its members to boycott the championships in protest.

Seventy-nine men withdrew their entries and only three ATP members played: Roger Taylor (GB), Ilie Nastase (Romania) and Ray Keldie (Australia). The ATP flexed its muscles in a significant trial of strength but, despite the absence of so many leading men, Wimbledon attracted over 300,000 spectators.

Jan Kodes, of Czechoslovakia, won the men's title in that turbulent episode. This period also yielded John Newcombe, Stan Smith, Jimmy Connors and Arthur Ashe as men's champions while the women's singles produced titleholders of the calibre of the uncrushable Billie Jean King, the unflappable Chris Evert Lloyd and the uncompromising Martina Navratilova.

Venues/3

However, the player of the 1970s was Bjorn Borg. Few tennis players have aroused public interest as emphatically as the stoic Swede who won Wimbledon five successive times from 1976 and captured the French title six times. Borg's loss of appetite for the pressures of tournament competition led to his retirement in 1983 at the age of 26. John McEnroe, the American with the saintly shots and satanic temper, wrested the Wimbledon title from the Swedish player's grasp in 1981, was beaten in the 1982 final by a resurgent Connors and regained the crown in 1983.

John Newcombe: two Wimbledon singles.

Jimmy Connors: resurgent.

People in the media

Dan Maskell
Dan Maskell is Britain's voice of tennis. Arthur Ashe, the 1975 Wimbledon champion, once said: 'If I woke up at 4am in Timbuktu in a fever and heard the inimitable voice of Dan Maskell I would know I was listening to a Wimbledon broadcast on the BBC.'

He was born in 1907 and has been commentating at Wimbledon since 1951 and has not missed a day at the championships since 1929. In his playing days he won the British professional title sixteen times. As a coach he was attached to the All England Club from 1929 until 1955. He was a Squadron Leader in the Royal Air Force during the Second World War when he was awarded the OBE for his work in the rehabilitation of wounded airmen.

John Barrett
John Barrett, a regular member of BBC TV's tennis commentary team, is a former British Davis Cup player and captain. He ran the LTA training squad — 'the Barrett Boys' — from 1965 to 1968. Apart from broadcasting, John, who was born in 1931, is a director of Slazengers and tennis correspondent of the *Financial Times*. He is married to former Wimbledon champion (1961) Angela Mortimer.

Mark Cox
Mark Cox has the credentials to provide expert analysis in his role as a TV commentator. A former British number one, he played in 16 Davis Cup ties, winning 15 out of 21 singles and 8 out of 14 doubles. He was born in Leicester in 1943 and educated at Millfield and Cambridge University, where he gained a degree in economics.

Ann Jones
Ann Jones brings a wealth of playing and administrative experience to her

John Barrett: Davis Cup experience.

TV commentating. The former British number one won the Wimbledon title in 1969, beating Margaret Court in the semi-finals and Billie Jean King in the final, and captured the French title in 1961 and 1966. She is now the Director of European Operations for the Women's Tennis Association.

Gerald Williams

Gerald Williams, who became BBC Radio's first full-time tennis correspondent 10 years ago, was born at Upper Norwood in 1929 in a house overlooking the courts where Bunny Austin and Roger Becker started their tennis. He worked on the *Croydon Advertiser,* the *Leicester Mercury* and the *South Wales Echo* before joining the *Daily Mail* and ultimately becoming the paper's tennis correspondent. After leaving the *Mail* he was a tennis and soccer commentator on independent TV and, through the Bagenal Harvey organisation, was involved in pioneering work in the commercial field for the LTA and subsequently the Wimbledon championships.

Dan Maskell with Virginia Wade.

Mark Cox: expert analyst.

Ann Jones: wealth of knowledge.

Statistics

Wimbledon champions

In the years before 1922 the holder did not compete in the championships but met the winner of the singles in the Challenge Round. This system was abolished in 1922 and the holder subsequently played through. Modified seeding was introduced in 1924 and full seeding in 1927. Wimbledon became Open in 1968.

Men's singles
1968	R. G. Laver
1969	R. G. Laver
1970	J. D. Newcombe
1971	J. D. Newcombe
1972*	S. R. Smith
1973*	J. Kodes
1974	J. S. Connors
1975	A. R. Ashe
1976	B. Borg
1977	B. Borg
1978	B. Borg
1979	B. Borg
1980	B. Borg
1981	J. P. McEnroe
1982	J. S. Connors
1983	J. P. McEnroe

Women's singles
1968	Mrs L. W. King
1969	Mrs P. F. Jones
1970*	Mrs B. M. Court
1971	Miss E. Goolagong
1972	Mrs L. W. King
1973	Mrs L. W. King
1974	Miss C. M. Evert
1975	Mrs L. W. King
1976*	Miss C. M. Evert
1977	Miss S. V. Wade
1978	Miss M. Navratilova
1979	Miss M. Navratilova
1980	Mrs R. A. Cawley
1981	Mrs J. M. Lloyd
1982	Miss M. Navratilova
1983	Miss M. Navratilova

Men's doubles
1968	J. D. Newcombe and A. D. Roche
1969	J. D. Newcombe and A. D. Roche
1970	J. D. Newcombe and A. D. Roche
1971	R. Emerson and R. G. Laver
1972	R. A. J. Hewitt and F. D. McMillan
1973	J. S. Connors and I. Nastase
1974	J. D. Newcombe and A. D. Roche
1975	V. Gerulaitis and A. Mayer
1976	B. E. Gottfried and R. Ramírez
1977	R. L. Case and G. Masters
1978	R. A. J. Hewitt and F. D. McMillan
1979	P. Fleming and J. P. McEnroe
1980	P. McNamara and P. McNamee
1981	P. Fleming and J. P. McEnroe
1982	P. McNamara and P. McNamee
1983	P. Fleming and J. P. McEnroe

Women's doubles
1968	R. Casals and L. W. King
1969	B. M. Court and J. A. M. Tegart
1970	R. Casals and L. W. King
1971	R. Casals and L. W. King
1972	L. W. King and B. F. Stove
1973	R. Casals and L. W. King
1974	E. Goolagong and P. Michel
1975	A. Kiyomura and K. Sawamatsu
1976	C. Evert and M. Navratilova
1977	H. Gourlay-Cawley and J. C. Russell
1978	G. E. Reid and W. Turnbull
1979	L. W. King and M. Navratilova
1980	K. Jordan and A. E. Smith
1981	M. Navratilova and P. H. Shriver
1982	M. Navratilova and P. H. Shriver
1983	M. Navratilova and P. H. Shriver

Mixed doubles
1968	K. N. Fletcher and Mrs B. M. Court
1969	F. S. Stolle and Mrs P. F. Jones
1970	I. Nastase and Miss R. Casals
1971	O. K. Davidson and Mrs L. W. King
1972	I. Nastase and Miss R. Casals
1973	O. K. Davidson and Mrs L. W. King
1974	O. K. Davidson and Mrs L. W. King
1975	M. C. Riessen and Mrs B. M. Court
1976	A. D. Roche and Miss F. Durr
1977	R. A. J. Hewitt and Miss G. R. Stevens
1978	F. D. McMillan and Miss B. F. Stove
1979	R. A. J. Hewitt and Miss G. R. Stevens
1980	J. R. Austin and Miss T. Austin
1981	F. D. McMillan and Miss B. F. Stove
1982	K. Curren and Miss A. E. Smith
1983	J. M. Lloyd and Miss W. M. Turnbull

* Holders did not defend title

US Open champions

Played at West Side Club, Forest Hills, New York on grass 1968–74, and on Har-Tru courts 1975–77. Played at the National Tennis Centre, Flushing Meadow, New York on cement from 1978 onwards.

Men's singles
1968   A. R. Ashe
1969   R. G. Laver
1970   K. R. Rosewall
1971   S. R. Smith
1972   I. Nastase
1973   J. D. Newcombe
1974   J. S. Connors
1975   M. Orantes
1976   J. S. Connors
1977   G. Vilas
1978   J. S. Connors
1979   J. P. McEnroe
1980   J. P. McEnroe
1981   J. P. McEnroe
1982   J. S. Connors
1983   J. S. Connors

Women's singles
1968   Miss S. V. Wade
1969   Mrs B. M. Court
1970   Mrs B. M. Court
1971   Mrs L. W. King
1972   Mrs L. W. King
1973   Mrs B. M. Court
1974   Mrs L. W. King
1975   Miss C. M. Evert
1976   Miss C. M. Evert
1977   Miss C. M. Evert
1978   Miss C. M. Evert
1979   Miss T. A. Austin
1980   Mrs J. M. Lloyd
1981   Miss T. A. Austin
1982   Mrs J. M. Lloyd
1983   Miss M. Navratilova

Men's doubles
1968   R. C. Lutz and S. R. Smith
1969   K. R. Rosewall and F. S. Stolle
1970   P. Barthès and N. Pilic
1971   J. D. Newcombe and R. Taylor
1972   E. C. Drysdale and R. Taylor
1973   J. D. Newcombe and O. K. Davidson
1974   R. C. Lutz and S. R. Smith
1975   J. S. Connors and I. Nastase
1976   M. C. Riessen and T. S. Okker
1977   R. A. J. Hewitt and F. D. McMillan
1978   R. C. Lutz and S. R. Smith
1979   J. P. McEnroe and P. Fleming
1980   R. C. Lutz and S. R. Smith
1981   J. P. McEnroe and P. Fleming
1982   K. Curren and S. Denton
1983   J. P. McEnroe and P. Fleming

Women's doubles
1968   M. E. Bueno and B. M. Court
1969   F. Durr and D. R. Hard
1970   B. M. Court and D. Dalton
1971   R. Casals and D. Dalton
1972   F. Durr and B. F. Stove
1973   B. M. Court and S. V. Wade
1974   R. Casals and Mrs L. W. King
1975   B. M. Court and S. V. Wade
1976   L. Boshoff and I. Kloss
1977   M. Navratilova and B. F. Stove
1978   M. Navratilova and L. W. King
1979   B. F. Stove and W. Turnbull
1980   M. Navratilova and L. W. King
1981   K. Jordan and A. E. Smith
1982   R. Casals and W. M. Turnbull
1983   M. Navratilova and P. Shriver

Mixed doubles
1968   Not held
1969   M. C. Riessen and Mrs B. M. Court
1970   M. C. Riessen and Mrs B. M. Court
1971   O. K. Davidson and Mrs L. W. King
1972   M. C. Riessen and Mrs B. M. Court
1973   O. K. Davidson and Mrs L. W. King
1974   G. Masters and Miss P. Teeguarden
1975   R. Stockton and Miss R. Casals
1976   P. Dent and Mrs L. W. King
1977   F. D. McMillan and Miss B. F. Stove
1978   F. D. McMillan and Miss B. F. Stove
1979   R. A. J. Hewitt and Miss G. R. Stevens
1980   M. C. Reissen and Miss W. M. Turnbull
1981   K. Curren and Miss A. E. Smith
1982   K. Curren and Miss A. E. Smith
1983   J. Fitzgerald and Miss E. Sayers

French Open champions

Men's singles
1968   K. R. Rosewall
1969   R. G. Laver
1970   J. Kodes
1971   J. Kodes
1972   A. Gimeno
1973   I. Nastase

Statistics/2

1974	B. Borg
1975	B. Borg
1976	A. Panatta
1977	G. Vilas
1978	B. Borg
1979	B. Borg
1980	B. Borg
1981	B. Borg
1982	M. Wilander
1983	Y. Noah

Women's singles

1968	Miss N. Richey
1969	Mrs B. M. Court
1970	Mrs B. M. Court
1971	Miss E. Goolagong
1972	Mrs L. W. King
1973	Mrs B. M. Court
1974	Miss C. M. Evert
1975	Miss C. M. Evert
1976	Miss S. Barker
1977	Miss M. Jausovec
1978	Miss V. Ruzici
1979	Mrs J. M. Lloyd
1980	Mrs J. M. Lloyd
1981	Miss H. Mandlikova
1982	Miss M. Navratilova
1983	Mrs J. M. Lloyd

Men's doubles

1968	K. R. Rosewall and F. S. Stolle
1969	J. D. Newcombe and A. D. Roche
1970	I. Nastase and I. Tiriac
1971	A. R. Ashe and M. C. Reissen
1972	R. A. J. Hewitt and F. D. McMillan
1973	J. D. Newcombe and T. S. Okker
1974	R. D. Crealy and O. Parun
1975	B. Gottfried and R. Ramírez
1976	F. McNair and S. Stewart
1977	B. Gottfried and R. Ramírez
1978	A. Mayer and H. Pfister
1979	A. Mayer and G. Mayer
1980	V. Amaya and H. Pfister
1981	H. Gunthardt and B. Taroczy
1982	S. Stewart and F. Taygan
1983	A. Jarryd and H. Simonsson

Women's doubles

1968	F. Durr and P. F. Jones
1969	F. Durr and P. F. Jones
1970	F. Durr and G. Chanfreau
1971	F. Durr and G. Chanfreau
1972	L. W. King and B. F. Stove
1973	B. M. Court and S. V. Wade
1974	C. M. Evert and O. Morozova
1975	C. M. Evert and M. Navratilova
1976	F. Bonicelli and G. Lovera
1977	R. Marsikova and P. Teeguarden
1978	M. Jausovec and V. Ruzici
1979	B. F. Stove and W. M. Turnbull
1980	K. Jordan and A. E. Smith
1981	R. Fairbank and T. Harford
1982	M. Navratilova and A. E. Smith
1983	R. Fairbanks and C. Reynolds

Mixed doubles

1968	J. C. Barclay and Miss F. Durr
1969	M. C. Riessen and Mrs B. M. Court
1970	R. A. J. Hewitt and Mrs L. W. King
1971	J. C. Barclay and Miss F. Durr
1972	K. Warwick and Miss E. Goolagong
1973	J. C. Barclay and Miss F. Durr
1974	I. Molina and Miss M. Navratilova
1975	T. Koch and Miss F. Bonicelli
1976	K. Warwick and Miss I. Koch
1977	J. P. McEnroe and Miss M. Carillo
1978	P. Slozil and Miss R. Tomanova
1979	R. A. J. Hewitt and Miss W. M. Turnbull
1980	W. Martin and Miss A. E. Smith
1981	J. Arias and Miss A. Jaeger
1982	J. M. Lloyd and Miss W. M. Turnbull
1983	E. Teltscher and Miss B. Jordan

Australian Open champions

Men's singles

1968	W. W. Bowrey
1969	R. G. Laver
1970	A. R. Ashe
1971	K. R. Rosewall
1972	K. R. Rosewall
1973	J. D. Newcombe
1974	J. S. Connors
1975	J. D. Newcombe
1976	M. Edmundson
1977 (Jan)	R. Tanner
1977 (Dec)	V. Gerulaitis
1978	G. Vilas
1979	G. Vilas
1980	B. Teacher
1981	J. Kriek
1982	J. Kriek

Women's singles

1968	Mrs L. W. King
1969	Mrs B. M. Court
1970	Mrs B. M. Court

1971	Mrs B. M. Court		1971	B. M. Court and E. Goolagong
1972	Miss S. V. Wade		1972	H. Gourlay and K. Harris
1973	Mrs B. M. Court		1973	B. M. Court and S. V. Wade
1974	Miss E. Goolagong		1974	E. Goolagong and P. Michel
1975	Miss E. Goolagong		1975	E. Goolagong and P. Michel
1976	Mrs R. A. Cawley		1976	E. Cawley and H. Gourlay
1977 (Jan)	Mrs G. Reid		1977 (Jan)	D. Fromholtz and H. Gourlay
1977 (Dec)	Mrs R. A. Cawley		1977 (Dec)	E. Cawley and H. Cawley divided with M. Guerrant and G. Reid
1978	Miss C. O'Neil			
1979	Miss B. Jordan			
1980	Miss H. Mandlikova		1978	B. Nagelsen and R. Tomanova
1981	Miss M. Navratilova		1979	J. Chaloner and D. Evers
1982	Mrs J. M. Lloyd		1980	B. Nagelsen and M. Navratilova
			1981	K. Jordan and A. E. Smith
			1982	M. Navratilova and P. H. Shriver

Men's doubles

1968	R. D. Crealy and A. J. Stone
1969	R. Emerson and R. G. Laver
1970	R. Lutz and S. R. Smith
1971	J. D. Newcombe and A. D. Roche
1972	K. R. Rosewall and O. K. Davidson
1973	J. D. Newcombe and M. J. Anderson
1974	R. Case and G. Masters
1975	J. D. Alexander and P. Dent
1976	J. D. Newcombe and A. D. Roche
1977 (Jan)	A. R. Ashe and A. D. Roche
1977 (Dec)	R. O. Ruffels and A. J. Stone
1978	W. Fibak and K. Warwick
1979	P. McNamara and P. McNamee
1980	M. Edmondson and K. Warwick
1981	M. Edmondson and K. Warwick
1982	J. D. Alexander and J. Fitzgerald

Mixed doubles

1968	R. D. Crealy and Mrs L. W. King
1969–82	Not held

WCT final winners

1971	K. R. Rosewall
1972	K. R. Rosewall
1973	S. R. Smith
1974	J. D. Newcombe
1975	A. R. Ashe
1976	B. Borg
1977	J. S. Connors
1978	V. Gerulaitis
1979	J. P. McEnroe
1980	J. S. Connors
1981	J. P. McEnroe
1982	I. Lendl
1983	J. P. McEnroe

Women's doubles

1968	K. M. Krantzcke and K. Melville
1969	B. M. Court and J. A. M. Tegart
1970	B. M. Court and J. Dalton

Davis Cup

Final rounds

1972	Bucharest	US	beat	Romania	3–2
1973*	Cleveland, Ohio	Australia	beat	US	5–0
1974*	—	South Africa	beat	India	w.o.
1975*	Stockholm	Sweden	beat	Czechoslovakia	3–2
1976*	Santiago	Italy	beat	Chile	4–1
1977*	Sydney	Australia	beat	Italy	3–1
1978*	Palm Springs	US	beat	GB	4–1
1979	San Francisco	US	beat	Italy	5–0
1980*	Prague	Czechoslovakia	beat	Italy	4–1
1981*	Cincinnati	US	beat	Argentina	3–1
1982	Grenoble	US	beat	France	4–1

* Holders beaten

Statistics/3

Grand Prix Masters

		Singles	Doubles
1970	Tokyo	S. R. Smith	R. G. Laver and J. Kodes
1971	Paris	I. Nastase	Not held
1972	Barcelona	I. Nastase	Not held
1973	Boston	I. Nastase	Not held
1974	Melbourne	G. Vilas	Not held
1975	Stockholm	I. Nastase	J. Gisbert and M. Orantes
1976	Houston	M. Orantes	F. McNair and S. Stewart
1977*	New York	J. S. Connors	R. A. J. Hewitt and F. D. McMillan
1978*	New York	J. P. McEnroe	P. Fleming and J. P. McEnroe
1979*	New York	B. Borg	P. Fleming and J. P. McEnroe
1980*	New York	B. Borg	P. Fleming and J. P. McEnroe
1981*	New York	I. Lendl	P. Fleming and J. P. McEnroe
1982	New York	I. Lendl	P. Fleming and J. P. McEnroe

* Played in January of the following year

Wightman Cup

1923	Forest Hills	US	7–0	1957	Pittsburgh	US	6–1
1924	Wimbledon	GB	6–1	1958	Wimbledon	GB	4–3
1925	Forest Hills	GB	4–3	1959	Pittsburgh	US	4–3
1926	Wimbledon	US	4–3	1960	Wimbledon	GB	4–3
1927	Forest Hills	US	5–2	1961	Chicago	US	6–1
1928	Wimbledon	GB	4–3	1962	Wimbledon	US	4–3
1929	Forest Hills	US	4–3	1963	Cleveland	US	6–1
1930	Wimbledon	GB	4–3	1964	Wimbledon	US	5–2
1931	Forest Hills	US	5–2	1965	Cleveland	US	5–2
1932	Wimbledon	US	4–3	1966	Wimbledon	US	4–3
1933	Forest Hills	US	4–3	1967	Cleveland	US	6–1
1934	Wimbledon	US	5–2	1968	Wimbledon	GB	4–3
1935	Forest Hills	US	4–3	1969	Cleveland	US	5–2
1936	Wimbledon	US	4–3	1970	Wimbledon	US	4–3
1937	Forest Hills	US	6–1	1971	Cleveland	US	4–3
1938	Wimbledon	US	5–2	1972	Wimbledon	US	5–2
1939	Forest Hills	US	5–2	1973	Boston	US	5–2
1940–5	Not held			1974	Deeside, Wales	GB	6–1
1946	Wimbledon	US	7–0	1975	Cleveland	GB	5–2
1947	Forest Hills	US	7–0	1976	Crystal Palace, London	US	5–2
1948	Wimbledon	US	6–1				
1949	Philadelphia	US	7–0	1977	Oakland, Cal.	US	7–0
1950	Wimbledon	US	7–0	1978	Albert Hall, London	GB	4–3
1951	Brookline, Mass.	US	6–1	1979	West Palm Beach	US	7–0
1952	Wimbledon	US	7–0	1980	Albert Hall, London	US	5–2
1953	Forest Hills	US	7–0	1981	Chicago	US	7–0
1954	Wimbledon	US	*6–0	1982	London	US	6–1
1955	Rye, NY	US	6–1	1983	Williamsburg	US	6–1
1956	Wimbledon	US	5–2				

* One rubber unplayed